FROM
TROUBLED
TIMES

by Howard E. Krehbiel

D0862449

Cover Photograph

Looking into the yard of the "Ulis" home in Weierhof, Germany; it was this home in 1792 that Grandfather Heinrich Krehbiel held the attention of his grandchildren as he told them how his own grandfather, Peter Krehbiel, was forced to leave his home in Switzerland in 1671, and settle at Weierhof in 1682.

Published by
Masthof Press
219 Mill Road
Morgantown, PA 19543-9701

PREFACE

This is a grandfather's story of interest to historians of Swiss Anabaptist traditions and to genealogists. It may fascinate especially those people whose Anabaptist ancestors, whether Mennonite or Amish, were forced to leave their homeland because of their faith. The grandfather of this story, who in 1792 is describing his own grandfather to his grandchildren, lived at that time in the house built by his own father, Michael Krehbiel I. Michael's initials and date {M 1712 K} carved on an outer beam were uncovered in recent times during refurbishing of this home. This Michael Krehbiel was the youngest of five known sons of the Peter Krehbiel I who was forced to leave Switzerland by 1671 and who settled at the Weierhof in the Palatinate of Germany in 1682. The story-telling grandfather was Heinrich Krehbiel, whose home in the community of Weierhof is still known as "Ulis" (with the U and i pronounced like bootie or newly). The name refers to Heinrich's son, Ulrich Krehbiel, who took over that home, and whose family is involved in later parts of this sequence of stories and letters.

Tracing family connections of that period is a challenge. By combining major contributions of many others, especially Adolph Hertzler of Gundheimerhof, near Weierhof in Germany, I have compiled a fairly complete genealogy of descendants of Peter Krehbiel I. It is comparable to that done in the early part of this century by J. J. Krehbiel on descendants of Jost Krehbiel I of the Pfrimmerhof, and that done in the 1940s by Paul Hirschler on descendants of Samuel Grehbill /Krebill of Altleiningen. These three villages are not far from each other in the Palatinate.

One of the challenges to genealogists is to establish with some certainty of documentation whatever connection may exist between these three and other progenitors of so many Krehbiel and Krebill families in America and in Germany. Many people have been working on this for many years, for which I am deeply grateful.

My own interest is partially motivated by the fact that I am a descendant of four of the five known sons of this Peter, and have established at least nine different ancestral lines leading from me to Peter. A number of lines trace back to Jost Krehbiel of the nearby Pfrimmerhof, and one line connects me to Samuel Krebill of Altleiningen.

The original form of this paper may be found under the title, "Aus Trüben Zeiten " in Jacob Ellenberger's *Bilder aus dem Pilgerleben*, part III, published in Stuttgart, 1883. This translation was done primar-ily in 1982 by Herman Neff of Cambridge, Ontario, Canada, with some portions begun earlier by Geert Balzer of Hamburg, Germany, when he was a student at Bluffton College. The poem about leaving Switzerland was originally translated by Delbert Gratz of Bluffton, Ohio. I am responsible for other editing, a complete comparison of the whole translation with Ellenberger's work, and its possible errors of translation and printing.

Jakob Ellenberger II [Aug. 2, 1831-Feb. 5, 1901] was a minister of the Mennonite congregation at Friedelsheim in Rheinland-Pfalz, and had no children. He succeeded his uncle, Jakob Ellenberger I, at Friedelsheim. He recorded many narratives about Mennonite families in his region. Ellenberger retells family stories in this article with great care for correctness of detail. His footnotes list other references and also some comments that portions are from actual documents and that others are from stories often repeated by others.

In working on this story, I have sought to determine what parts are factual and what is legend. Some parts were easily verified while others will need further research. For example, the earliest writings that Ellenberger says he is copying, said to be by Peter Krehbiel, I have not been able to locate. However, I was granted the privilege to photocopy all the letters by Heinrich Krehbiel, one of the grandchildren listening to the stories by his grandfather Heinrich. I also photocopied many of the earliest inheritable lease documents [Erbbeständ Brief] to be found in homes at the Weierhof. It is possible that the other documents may still be in other homes there, where people of the community have carefully kept paper and parchment documents over the centuries.

A puzzling item is the first poem. Some of it, which is given in colloquial Swiss, is said to have been written in prison in 1670 in Bern by the same Peter Krehbiel who in 1682 obtained the inheritance lease of the Weierhof farm in the Palatinate. It closely resembles a similar poem written about Hans of Haslibach who was beheaded in prison in Switzerland in 1571. But which of these was written first, and who wrote them?

Harold S. Bender wrote in his *Mennonite Encyclopedia* article on Haslibach that the Haslibacher poem or song was found bound as an additional booklet, but was not printed with, an edition of the *Ausbund* that he decided was published in the early 17th century. Upon comparison, that copy of the *Ausbund* in the Mennonite Historical Library at Goshen, Indiana, resembles closely another early one that exists in the Mennonite Historical Library at Bluffton College. Neither of these has any indication of publisher, location, or date.

The copy at Bluffton, like the one at Goshen, has bound with the *Ausbund* the separately printed pamphlet containing the Haslibacher poem. One of the songs of the *Ausbund* portion tells about the execution of Hans Landis in 1614, so that copy of the *Ausbund* was printed after 1614, but has no publication data. The added pamphlet that includes the Haslibacher song has neither date, publisher, nor location, but has the descriptive comment that it relates the story of the 1571 imprisonment and death of Hans of Haslibach.

Still other pamphlets also bound into the volume at Bluffton have publication dates 1694 and 1695. Those portions attest to this binding of the Bluffton *Ausbund* with the several additional booklets after 1695. But even if only the first two undated sections were bound together in the edition of the Goshen *Ausbund* that Bender referred to, this oes not seem to support the contention that it was published in the early 17th century.

To my knowledge, this song/poem did not appear in any European edition of the *Ausbund* during that period, but did appear in all editions known to be published in America from 1742 onward, and all of those I have seen include the Haslibacher poem/song as number 140. It also is printed as a poem in some of the later (1748...) American editions of the *Martyrs Mirror.*

Christian Neff, an influential minister-historian at the Weierhof, was a major writer of the German predecessor to the *Mennonite Encyclopedia,* the *Mennonitische Lexikon.* He notes that the Haslibacher poem/song first appeared around 1670, had 32 verses in one version, but only 12 verses in another version. He also provided several references.

Although the Haslibacher poem has the same wording as the Krehbiel poem in the parts that are comparable the Haslibacher

v

poem has many additional verses. This raises the question as to which one is a copy and extension or reduction of the other. It was and still is common for artists in many fields to borrow themes to rework into something suited to their own purposes. The later invention often turn out to be the more widely known. I had hoped to determine whether the Haslibacher poem was written before the suggested 1670 date of the Peter Krehbiel poem about his father. This I have not been able to do. John Oyer of Goshen suggested that this may not be achievable until one can obtain more conclusive analysis of date and place of comparable printing and binding of other works.

On other points, though persecution forced many Swiss people to leave their homeland in 1671, and there are a number of Krähenbühl individuals who were called to Bern at different times, I have not discovered specific records in the Bern Archives regarding an Anabaptist Krähenbühl in prison in Bern in 1670 or 1671. However, while working on the translation of this article in July 1978, I asked Delbert Gratz to read my manuscript. After doing so, he suggested that he bring out a detailed map of Zäziwil region to attempt to identify the Cräyenbühl farm and cemetery. Together we located the farm Kräbühl (spelled Cräjbüel on recent maps) located on a hill just south of Zäziwil. This confirmed part of the story that was being told.

An exploration of the old registration books of marriages [Eherodel] and baptisms [Taufrodel] for that area in those times does not clearly identify a Krähenbühl family that included the brothers Peter, Michael, and Jost as described in this story. Delbert Gratz makes the quite plausible suggestion that this could be due to the fact that Anabaptists did not take their young children to be baptized in the state church, and the state church would not record the adult baptisms. I found occasional notations in the old records that certain individuals in the Zäziwil community were "Anabaptist," or some other comment suggesting non-compliance with state church requirements for all citizens. All this makes more difficult the attempts to connect the known Peter Krehbiel at the Weierhof and the Jost Krehbiel at the Pfrimmerhof as possibly brothers from the Krähenbühl by Zäziwil.

I had hoped to document the early part of the story to distinguish between facts and legends. To date, this has not been possible. I invite readers to share in the settlement of these questions and to share new discoveries.

Most of Ellenberger's footnotes are translated and appear now as endnotes. Occasional comments by me are printed within square [brackets].

I have felt that the whole narrative should best be printed along with this preface as one document. This ties together the quandaries, motivations, and decisions that members of this representative Swiss-German Mennonite family experienced through a number of generations. To me it is a story about a Swiss Anabaptist family in the 1670s, being told to grandchildren in Germany in the 1790s, was first published in German in the 1880s, and was translated to English and republished in America by a descendant another hundred years later. It is surely a most intriguing tale to help our grandchildren know a little more about questions faced in earlier days, particularly those who share some form of heritage with individuals being described.

I want to give credit and heartfelt thanks to Lois Ann Mast and to David Habegger for their creative suggestions and inspiring encouragement that has made this publication possible.

Howard E. Krehbiel
September 1994

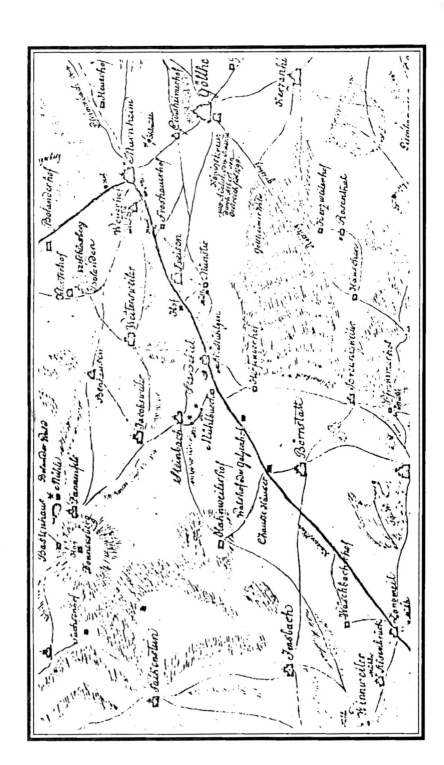

FROM TROUBLED TIMES

According to Old Papers and Stories
of a Grandfather

By Jacob Ellenberger and Translated by Howard E. Krehbiel

"Grandfather, there is going to be war, isn't there?" anxiously asked little Elizabeth of her grandfather, who was sitting in his roughly hewn high-back chair. He was wearing a short jacket and knee-length leather trousers.

"Yes, in France there are bad things happening," answered the grandfather. "Who knows what we will live to see in the next eight years until we write the year 1800." There was a short silence.

Let's look closer at the setting for this story. It is the larger room of a farmhouse. It is sparsely furnished and everything appears to be homemade. There is a strong oak table with crossed legs, a bench behind it, some chairs, and in the corner is a big canopy bed with green curtains and a high wooden border shelf on which there is a row of red apples. In the corner where the grandfather is sitting, there is a small cupboard on the wall with some books in it. The big book with the strong leather binding may attract our attention. If we opened it, we would find inscribed on the inside of the cover the following words written by a man's strong hand.

> *This Bible belongs to me, Heinrich Krehbiel, at the Weyerhof farm, and I bought it in the year 1759 and it cost 5 florins and 15 albus.* (One albus = two kreuzer.)

Map on preceding page: A handsketched map of a region in the Pfalz showing Weierhof in the upper right corner and Pfrimmerhof at the bottom in the middle. The map was drawn in 1850 by Jacob Krehbiel who had emigrated from Pfrimmerhof to Clarence Center, New York, in 1829.

1

"Do not torture yourself in distress and sadness,
Set your trust in God!
Many troubles might strike you;
Stand against any that won't go away.
Oh, be mindful of the end! Christian,
Be fearful of God! Be steadfast in childlike love.
Do not complain, even when pain and suffering surround you.
Be virtuous, and live as a good example at all times!"

An iron lamp, fixed to the wall with a nail, gives only a little light in the room. The grandmother, the mother, and the oldest daughter, Katharina, are busy turning their spinning wheels. The father of this home is sorting willow branches that he will use during the long winter evenings to make baskets and brooms for the household. Even the grandfather makes his growing grandchildren happy by sometimes making pretty little baskets and brooms for them.

After a while, the grandfather took the little girl aside and stroked her curly hair from her forehead. Smiling, he said, "Do you think you know what war means?"

"Yes, grandfather," she answered quickly, "in war people beat each other to death. Will I also be beaten to death, grandfather?" Tears welled up in her eyes.

But before he could answer, the oldest, the nine-year-old son named Heinrich like his grandfather, stood at his side and asked, "Have you ever been in a war?"

"No, I haven't, thank heavens. But my grandfather knew what war was, and he used to talk about it a lot."

"Your grandfather was chased out of Switzerland, wasn't he?" Heinrich pressed on.

"Yes, he was driven out of Switzerland some 120 years ago."

"Then your grandfather must have been a bad man, right? If he wasn't, he wouldn't have been chased out," said the little Susanna.

2

"No, children, my grandfather was a righteous, God-fearing man."

"Please tell us what you know about him," the children begged.

"I'll be glad to," said the grandfather. "Especially since I don't know whether I will be with you much longer. Tonight I'll read to you what my grandfather himself wrote down about his life."

While he was getting the document, the children pushed the easy chair closer to the light and gathered around it. The spinners also came closer so they would not miss anything. Soon the grandfather came back. He opened a big yellowish paper, laid a smaller piece of paper on the table in front of himself, and started to read:

What I, Peter Cräyenbühl, Have Experienced

I was born in Switzerland, in the territory of Bern. It was not far from the Aar River where my father's house stood. It was a beautiful farmhouse, surrounded by beautiful fruit trees. Our farm was located in the

Zäziwil in the foreground with the Krähenbühl farm in the top center among the trees not far from the large dark forest to the left. Credit: Howard E. Krehbiel.

3

Village of Zäziwil, Switzerland, today. The Krehbiel family fled from here in 1671. Courtesy: David Habegger.

village of Zäziwil. My mother died early and my father raised my two brothers and me, without getting married again.

We were brought up to fear God and to read the Bible diligently. We worked in our fields, and we didn't concern ourselves about other things very much. We met with our fellow believers on Sundays, sometimes here, sometimes there, for devotions with one another from God's word. We lived widely dispersed, some in the Emmental, others in the Simmental, some also in the Haslital. Many of the others were farmers as we were, but there were also some craftsmen in our group, especially weavers and woodcarvers. We never wronged anyone, and everybody kept to his own business.

4

Then in the year of our Lord 1670 persecution broke out again. People called us heretics and verbally abused us everywhere. We practiced witchcraft, they said, and had a pact with the devil. We were able to endure that because we knew ourselves to be innocent in our own conscience. Soon, however, many were imprisoned and were badly treated; they were supposed to renounce their beliefs.

Our father too went to prison in the city of Bern. Our begging and pleading was in vain. We affirmed repeatedly that he was innocent. Our distress was great. We sought help from the neighbors, but everywhere we found the same trouble. Our father was considered the leading heretic, and trickery and violence was used on him. Nevertheless, he remained true to his beliefs.

One day an armed government police officer came to us again and announced bluntly that he "had orders

The Krähenbühl farmhouse near Zäziwil, Switzerland, is spelled Cräjbüel on current maps. Credit: Howard E. Krehbiel.

to throw me into prison immediately."* When I replied to him, "Keep calm, good friend, that's no way to treat a human being," he said, "I don't like it either, but the high officials down in Bern have said that you are to come with me at once."

I saw that this man was following his instructions only reluctantly. Therefore I said to him, "You certainly don't want to go down to Bern without something to eat; so let's first have a cup of something warm together."

In this way I too went to Bern to be imprisoned. There I heard how my poor father was mistreated and tortured, but I heard also how he was miraculously set free and that he went back home. While in prison, I wrote the following song about these events:

A Spiritual Song

about Jost Cräyenbühl [Krähenbühl] of the village of Zäziwil in Switzerland, as he was set free from prison on the 15th day of the month of Lent, anno domini 1671. (To the melody of "Why are you full of sorrow, my heart?")[1]

1) What causes us to begin to sing about an old man who was from the Cräyenbühl? He was also called Cräyenbühl, from the village of Zäziwil.

2) God permitted it to happen that he was accused for the sake of his beliefs, so that he was imprisoned in the city of Bern.

---

*Ellenberger gave this conversation in the Bernese-German dialect, but provided a translation in standard High German in footnotes not given here.

3) And when in captivity, he was tormented and tortured severely for the sake of his faith; but he remained steadfast in his torture, fear, and pain.

4) On a Friday, as I was given to understand, the learned men visited him at the prison to debate with him, that he should turn from his beliefs.

5) The Cräyenbühler, instead of getting involved in the disputation, soon spoke to them of his unyielding faith, and that he was prepared to sacrifice his body and life for his beliefs.

6) And because it was approaching Sunday, the learned men became insistent and warned him that he must revoke his beliefs or his head would be cut off.

7) Very soon he gave the answer to them: "I shall not move away from my beliefs; I will hold to them firmly because my beliefs are right before God, and He will protect me."

8) And then Saturday night approached. And an angel of God came with might, near to the Cräyenbühler. He spoke: "God has sent me to you, to comfort you in your misery.

9) "And further I command you: Do not be moved away from your faith, but remain strong and firm, because your beliefs are right in the eyes of God, and He will watch over your soul.

10) "When people severely threaten you that they will execute you by the sword, do not be afraid; I will stand by your side, they will not harm you."

11) And then it was on Monday when the learned men came once again to visit the Cräyenbühler to argue with him, saying, "You must turn away from your beliefs."

12) "If not," they said as their last warning, "you will suffer death tomorrow." The Cräyenbühler spoke: "Rather than I deny my beliefs, I would let my head be cut off."

13) So one of them took him to the guest house restaurant and put before him food and drink, with the executioner seated next to him so that he should become fearful and yet turn away from his beliefs.

14) And when the meal was ended, one wanted to bind his hands, but the Cräyenbühler said: "I beg of you, Master Lorentz, that you would let me be unbound."

15) Herewith he fell on his knees and prayed the Lord's Prayer once or twice. When finished with his prayer, he declared that he was at peace with God and if God willed it, he would be delivered from his misery.

16) Then an angel appeared and took him by his hand. The angel's garment was nothing but light. The people were trembling in fear, as the angel guided the faithful one into his house.

17) Then the people said that God's will had been fulfilled, and they were in great fear. They said, "If we will leave him alone, God will be more pleased with us."

18) Gone then was the pain of torture, and he continued to live a strong and faithful life. And in the end God freed him from all his burdens and took him up to Himself in Heaven.

19) The writer of this song was a son of Cräyenbühl, a prisoner himself, when feather and ink were made available to him. God grant us a good rest for the night.

Grandfather continued to read what Peter had written:

Many readied themselves then for emigration. We also sold our farm, the Cräyenbühl, but did not get much for it. We were three brothers: Michel, Jost, and I, Peter. We divided our few possessions amongst ourselves. It deeply hurt us when we had to leave our father's house, our home. For a long time we stood on the hillside near the village and looked back. I thought then that my heart must break for the unspeakable hurt. Only then I knew how beautiful it was in my homeland. There was my father's house, so quiet and peaceful, with meadows spread around it, where we had worked by the sweat of our brows. Nearby there was the cemetery, where our dear parents were resting until the day of resurrection. And in the background rose up the Alps, covered forever with snow. Perhaps that was the same as Abraham felt when the Lord said to him: "Leave your people and your friends." I also put my trust in the God of Abraham when I heard those words from my heart: "I will lead you to a new land."

So we wandered toward this unknown land with confidence. I must confess that I was richly blessed by the grace of our God. I was able, unworthy as I was, to speak with the apostle who said: "We are troubled on every side, yet not distressed; we are perplexed, but not in despair; persecuted, but not forsaken; cast down, but not destroyed." (II Corinthians, 4: 8, 9)

"I also would like to read to you," said the grandfather, reaching for the other piece of paper on the table, "a poem about the farewell to his homeland, written by a descendant of Peter Krehbiel."

PETER KREHBIEL'S
FAREWELL TO HIS HOMELAND

Farewell you Alps, you beloved countryside.
You homelike village in the quiet valley!
You beloved fields someone else will care for;
O fatherhouse, you I will no longer see,
May God watch over you! Farewell for the last time.

See how pleasantly one is greeted over there,
Glowing in the sun's first rays,
The snow-covered stern gigantic peaks:
The lofty Jungfrau, Eiger, Mönch, and Niesen;
You greet me for the last, the last time.

Farewell you valleys with steep rock walls
Severe and barren, that stretch to the heavens;
That send their streams from high above
That end in spray in the gorge.
Also to you I say farewell for the last, last time.

You bring me to tears no less today,
You forest-wreathed lakes, so bright as metal;
Where we happily sang in light canoes,
The disturbed surface soon frightened the swans;
I travel on you for the last, the last time.

There on the meadows I see slowly moving
The well-fed cattle in great numbers.
Do you hear the Alphorn sounding over there?
Do you hear the herdsmen resoundingly sing and yodel?
I hear you, ah! for the last, the last time.

Oh fatherhouse, your warm beloved rooms
Where I knew life's joy and pain,
Farewell, farewell, in the shade of your trees!
It breaks my heart to tarry longer.
Oh, farewell for the last, the last time.

Still one glance at my parents' grave,
There under the freshly-wreathed marker,
Where I felt a need to come to pray!
Now I, filled with grief, grip my wanderer's staff,
And greet even you for the last, last time.

And you who have persecuted me with fury and vengeance,
Nevertheless I ask that the grace of the Lord be upon you.
Do you think that I would permit my cherished beliefs
Of my Lord and Savior to be taken from me?
Also farewell to all of you for the last time.

Take everything away! Only leave me my Savior!
Earthly goods are only waste and husks.
In distress I am more fortunate than before;
The storming flood around me, I am on safe ground,
So I feel at peace now for the first time.

So farewell then to all! I must now depart.
Farewell! For me there is no other choice.
The Lord is indeed my shepherd, He will lead me
To fresh pastures; He will bring me, though through suffering,
Someday to break bread with Him.

It was a sad group of people on the move. We were approximately 700 people, and among these were families with 10 to 12 children. As long as we were in the Bern area, we were ridiculed and laughed at on our way. We had less trouble in the Jura mountains of the Bisthum of Basel. In the valley of Münster the people were friendly to us, gave us food and drink, and tried to help us in our difficult situation. Here some of our group found already a new homeland. The rest of us traveled through the valley of the Birs toward Basel. From there our ways parted. Some traveled through France in order to find their way by ship to America; others traveled down the Rhine to the Netherlands, where many of our fellow believers welcomed us with loving hearts. One other group made their way to the Alsace and to the Kurpfalz [Palatinate].

We brothers separated in Basel. My brother Michel joined the group going to America, to be with his bride and her parents. I never heard anything from him since. God rest his soul, if he is no longer living.

My youngest brother Jost and I wanted to go to the Palatinate. We had heard that the Kurfürst[2] Karl Ludwig would welcome Swiss immigrants. We therefore made our way there in the hope that we would find a new homeland. The further we went into Alsace, the more troubled we became.

Oh how different was the landscape from that of Switzerland. Back there we saw beautiful villages and waving fields of grain. The fat cattle lay comfortably in lush grass, and the people went merrily about their daily tasks.

Here, however, whole villages lay in ruins grown over by weeds. The fields were partly covered with thornbushes and hedges. It was so sad to see everywhere the traces of the great war. We also saw wolves in abundance. Two or three of these beasts we clubbed to death.

The misery during the war must have been terrible. People kept telling us about it. The Spanish and the Swedes and other warring people had been in the land; so many had died and there was terrible famine. For food they had to be satisfied with roots, grass, and tree leaves. If there was not enough of these things, then they would eat the dead animals; yes, even the decaying flesh from the gallows and the cemeteries was used for food. We were told that the dead bodies of children were not safe from the devouring desire of the parents

12

for food. And it is said that young girls had eaten in the open field the dead body of their playmate. Straying soldiers were looting in the streets, and marauders made a business of murdering. Friends would kill their friends in order to eagerly eat them. A clergyman in the Palatinate told me that he had seen how at a fallen horse, people, dogs, and ravens were all feeding themselves.

Nine-tenths of the population of the Palatinate[3] was believed to have perished from murder, pestilence, and starvation, and the once beautiful countryside of the Palatinate looked like a deserted graveyard.—

Oh, almighty eternal God, keep and protect us!

The grandfather folded the paper carefully and added: "Yes protect us from such evil times, dear God!"

"Is the story already finished?" asked Heinrich. "Didn't your grandfather write more about his life?"

"Yes," said the grandfather. "He had written more, but those papers were lost during the war."

"During which war?" inquired the children simultaneously. "Tell us more!"

"You see, children, your grandfather is tired, and it is time for you to go to bed," said the mother. "Perhaps he will continue with this story tomorrow."

"Yes, if God wills and we live, I will do it," said the grandfather.

Then the father stood up, took the large Bible from the corner cupboard, as well as Johann Arndt's *True Christianity*, and read one portion from each of these with everyone listening devoutly.

13

The next evening they all sat silently again around the grandfather and listened in suspense as he, sitting in the high-backed chair, continued his story.

"Last evening I read to you how and why my grandfather emigrated from Switzerland. Today I will tell you as well as I can remember how he settled here and how it went for him at first. I will also tell you how the French sinned against our land. You will then be better able to deal with your own future experiences, because God will not let such crying injustices go unpunished.

"You will remember that my grandfather found everywhere the traces of the great German war. Soon he was to experience war himself.

"In the Haardt mountains lived some of our fellow believers, who much earlier had migrated there from the Netherlands. From them my grandfather received counsel and support.

"When he had been there for two or three years the French invaded the Palatinate under Marshal Turenne. It was, I believe, in the summer of 1674. Everyone fled from this dreaded enemy because they laid to waste and destroyed whatever came into their way. Whole villages, which had been built up from the ruins under the wise reign of the good Kurfürst Karl Ludwig, were again being destroyed.[4]

"The Kurfürst saw from his castle how the dwellings of his subjects went up in flames, but he was not able to help. Yes, when the King of France took many of his villages after the Peace of Nimmweg[5] of 1678, the poor Kurfürst died of a heart attack.

"I do not know where my grandfather lived during that war, much less what happened to him. I do know, however, that he got married again. His second wife was called Anna, and she was also an emigrant from Switzerland. I have never heard what her maiden name was. It is now just a hundred years since they arrived here at the Weierhof. Kurfürst Karl had granted them the farm under a hereditary lease, but he did not walk in the footsteps of his predecessor, Karl Ludwig. He was said to be very stubborn and very wasteful.

14

The Weierhof Mill from the side where the diverted stream and mill wheel were once located. Credit: Howard E. Krehbiel.

"My grandparents had a very difficult beginning here. During the big war, the Weierhof had been destroyed completely. They found nothing but ruins which were overgrown by weeds. In the debris and ruins of the cemetery the bare walls of a little chapel stuck out. Not much better was the condition of the fields which had not seen a plow for half a century. It was much the same in the areas surrounding the Weierhof. Bennhausen, for example, was, as my grandfather often told, completely devasted and uninhabited at that time.[6] You can well imagine that much work had to be done. Just listen to a few things to which my grandfather had to obligate himself in that lease.

"First of all, he had to build a new house with stables and a barn. In addition to the high annual lease cost, he also had to provide 100 malter from the harvest 'for the improvement to be implemented, and to maintain the hereditary lease.' In case he would get behind in his lease payments for three years, then all his possessions and food, whether in storage or being harvested, would be taken from him. And that would include any property which he may have allocated to his

15

The home named "Ulis" where Grandfather Heinrich Krehbiel told his grand-children about his own grandfather, Peter Krehbiel. Credit: Howard E. Krehbiel.

The initials "M.K." carved and dated 1712 by Michael Krehbiel, youngest son of Peter Krehbiel who had settled at Weierhof in 1682. These initials were discovered during fairly recent renovation of this home that is still known as "Ulis" today, referring to Ulrich Krehbiel, grandson of Michael.

heirs, all of this to be returned to the Kurfürst. Nothing would protect the lessee:

> no rights, no excuses which he may think of now or in the future, including war, fire, hail, and bad harvests. His religion may be only observed privately with his children in his home, including prayer, and he may not attempt to include in his Anabaptist doings even his Anabaptist brethren working for him, or any other persons of the Anabaptist sect. These regulations apply, regardless under whatever kind of pretension he may gather these people around him, and in particular, he shall not attempt to form a congregation.

"Everything that annually had to be delivered to the storage places you could read for yourself in the lease document. To follow such stipulations and to fulfill the requirements truly required strength and a trust in God, both of which my grandfather possessed.

"With good courage he now set about his work. The remnants of the chapel were converted into a home, and after that he built a barn and a stable. At the same time, he cleaned the bushy growth from the better field and prepared it for seeding. With God's help they survived the first difficult years. Sometimes, after their necessary payments and deliveries for the lease, they hardly had left one malter to cover their own needs. They had already cleaned and prepared for cultivation the larger portion of the fields and were looking forward to a brighter future, when the French came again into the land. Louis XIV of France, the 'All-Christian King," as he would let himself be called, had issued the order that the entire Palatinate should be laid waste.

"That year of 1689 was a terrible one for the Palatinate. The stealing and murdering French were burning to ashes one city after the other. The inhabitants themselves were forced to help in the destruction of their own properties with their own hands. Many left the area, and alone from Mannheim 200 families moved away to the city of Magdeburg.

"More than 1,000 villages were leveled to the ground. The vineyards were torn out and the fruit trees were cut off. The idea was that there should be a wasteland between Germany and France. That was the order which was followed fully by the shameful action of the French. Far into the summer the Weierhof remained untouched. My grandparents, in fact, had some hope that the French murderers would not reach into this rather remote part of the Palatinate; but soon they did arrive.

"One evening, when they were about to retire, they heard steps in the farmyard. Quickly my grandfather rose when he heard heavy fists banging against the windows, and voices calling, 'Come out, come out! Right away!'

"'What's going on?' shouted my grandfather.

"'Quickly, quickly, the French are coming!'

"Now my grandfather recognized the cousin Danner from the Donnersberg. He had observed from his high grounds that the French were coming through the Zellerthal [Zell Valley], and in order to save his friends and brethren in the faith, he had hurried to help them.

"In no time the whole family were on their feet. Cousin Danner had already awakened the servants. The animals were loosened from their chains and the oxen were put in front of the wagon. Anything that one could find in a hurry was put in the wagon, and as it usually is in a confusion like that, many an unnecessary item was taken along, and more important things remained behind.

"Then everyone hurried as quickly as possible through the woods to the Donnersberg. The servants were urging the animals onward, and my grandfather was driving the oxen wagon. Cousin Danner carried one of the boys on his back and the other one was holding his hand. Grandmother followed on foot behind the wagon. She had the youngest child wrapped into her skirt and carried him in her arms. The two older brothers were walking beside her.

"There was a thunderstorm approaching from the Donnersberg. Lightning was slashing through the air, and the thunder resounded frightfully through the forested valley. Soon it was heavily raining. The animals bellowed, and only with great effort was it possible to urge them to go forward. My father was at that time only three years old, but he never forgot that night. How often would he tell us about his trip to the Donnersberg.

"Toward the morning they reached to the high grounds on the Donnersberg, and were received as friends. They were in safety, because the Donnersberg, including the entire community of Kirchheim, was a part of France and under French administration at that time. The All-Christian King had taken it on an impulse without reason from the government of Nassau soon after the Peace of 'Nymmweg.'[7]

"On the very same day they could see from the Donnersberg the approaching French. Their way was made visible through destroyed villages and burning cities. Heidelberg, Mannheim, Worms, Speier, Frankenthal, and Alzey had been destroyed from January to August of that year. Our refugees were fearing for the Weierhof, when they saw a detachment of horsemen branching off the main road towards the Weierhof. With tears in their eyes they had to witness how the buildings that had been so carefully erected and filled with some of the supplies from the fields now went up in flames. And nevertheless my grandfather often said that in spite of all the troubles, he felt the protection of his Lord so strongly, and never stronger since his immigration. When they looked down from the Hirtenfelsen [herder's lookout rocks], then the cousin Danner quoted the words from the Prophet Isaiah: 'Your land has been laid to waste, your cities have been burned; strangers are taking your fields from you and destroy everything;' and then he responded to himself with the words from Job: 'The Lord gave it, and the Lord took it.' And in a cheerful expression of faith he added, 'The Name of the Lord be praised!'

"The main body of the French troops, however, moved towards Bolanden. There they positioned their cannons in the direction of the castle which had looked down into the valley for many hundreds of years. And it disappeared into ruins. This castle had survived the Peasant Wars [1524/25], and it also survived the Great War [Thirty Years War from 1618 to 1648], and now it had to be destroyed by these robbers.

"Oh my children, you do not know how much France has sinned on Germany. Wherever you go in the Palatinate you will find these

19

destroyed castles, which will remind you of that time. And further down the Rhine, to the left and to the right, you can see those sad ruins looking down upon you. Where at one time cheerful lives prevailed and proud knights lived, there are only heaps of stones, visited only on occasions by a curious wanderer.

"I saw those ruins one time when I walked to Neuwied with cousin Adam.[8] You know that in earlier days he had also to preach there. Maybe he will tell you sometime what he had experienced during his travels to Neuwied and then to Mülheim where he visited our good friend Teerstegen. When cousin Adam showed me the ruins at that time, and told me their names, he also said, 'Woe to France, when the punishment of God will be coming upon it.' Now it seems that God is about to raise his staff to punish France. You will see wonderful things, my children; the Antichrist will come and persecute those who believe in Christ. But it will come about, probably in 1836, as the man of God, Bengel, has calculated from the Revelation of John, that the thousand year reign of Christ will begin, with the appearance of our Lord and Savior Jesus Christ. Therefore, my children, blessed be the man who can bear suffering, but will persevere to the end."

Grandfather was moved by his own words. Only after awhile he added, "I was also affected by my story, but it is enough for today anyway. Tomorrow, if God wills, I will continue."

"Grandfather, may I ask you something?" said Heinrich. "Where did Jost go, the brother of your grandfather?"

"We have no certain knowledge about him; perhaps it was he who moved at the beginning of our century to the Pfrimmerhof, because the first owner of the Pfrimmerhof was called Jost Krehbiel and came from Switzerland."

The following evening the grandfather continued his stories:

"Today I have read up on several things to enable me to tell you in more detail about the Mennonites and about the Protestants in general; what they had to suffer in those days to maintain their faith, and how our ancestors, under the current rule, were able to gradually improve their material existence and religious freedom.

"After several days the French moved away from our area and our people were able to return from the Donnersberg. They were cheerful and thankful that they had saved their lives and had a roof over their heads. The house, the former chapel, could still be lived in, though the windows had been smashed and tables and chairs had been broken to pieces. All the harvested crops were gone. With some of the grain they had fed the horses, and the rest was destroyed when the barn was burned down. What still was left in the fields was trampled on and was not usable from the rain on the soft soil. However, my grandparents did not despair; they remembered their landlord, Kurfürst Philipp Wilhelm, who was still poorer than they were. Heidelberg, with its beautiful castles, had been burned to the ground. The Kurfürst and his son-in-law fled to the Emperor Leopold in Vienna, where he soon died.

"The years that followed were still difficult years for the people at the Weierhof. It was perhaps even more difficult than the early years because they had to suffer much from the officials of the new Kurfürst, Johann Wilhelm, who was, like his predecessor, a Catholic. Kurfürst Johann Wilhelm had moved his residence to Düsseldorf, where he held court in a luxurious fashion and did all the things he liked to do, while at the same time the greater part of the Palatinate kept being devastated by the French for several more years.

"Behaving worse than anyone else were the Capuchin and Franciscan monks who had arrived in the country with the French. They took from the Protestants one church after the other. Anyone who did not want to become a Catholic was fined large sums of money. At the point of the bayonet, those who resisted were driven into the church. At the altar, the Host (the sacraments of the Lord's Supper) was quickly shoved into their mouths, and saying, "By this proof you now belong to the Catholic church! At other places,[9] anyone who would change to the Catholic faith received, by the order of Louis XIV, ten florins. Whoever would convert to Catholicism on his birthday even received a free drink. That is how the 'Most Christian' King was concerned about the salvation of his subjects. This was the treatment given to

21

the Protestants, and you can imagine that the poor Mennonites did not fare any better.

"I want to tell you about only one case of which I have good personal knowledge. Protestants were ordered, at the punishment of twenty Reichsthaler, to decorate their homes and to bow their knees when Catholics would pass by in procession. Cousin Schmidt in Gundersheim was living at that time with his brother-in-law Rupp. He was mentally ill and already 60 years old, and suffered from an illness which made it necessary that he should wear long women's clothes. The only thing he could do was to fetch water every day in a pitcher at the fountain. One time he met a procession, and because he did not bow his knees, he was beaten on his head with a stick so that he died several days later as the result of the injuries received.

"Many then, for all these reasons, again took up their walking sticks and emigrated, particularly to North America. A few left for Brandenburg,[10] where earlier the Huguenots, who had been driven out of France, had been given a friendly reception. The Mennonites who remained behind, in spite of all their suffering, remained faithful. They still had their Bibles from which they always could receive consolation and gain new strength in their faith.

"The Peace of Ryswick[11] at least made an end to the sufferings of war in the Palatinate. France had to return the land which it had conquered, but the persecution of the Protestants did not come to an end.[12] It was a peace which meant that everyone kept taking what he wanted from the oppressed. Only God knows what would have happened to the Protestants in the Palatinate if Kurfürst Friedrich III of Brandenburg, who then became King Friedrich I of Prussia, would not have intervened. Upon his urging, the Kurfürst Johann Wilhelm finally allowed free religious exercise.[13] Unfortunately, this was on paper only; in reality the persecution of the Protestants continued. During the severe winter of 1709 the inhabitants suffered terribly. There came word of a promise of help from some rich people in England that they would offer a home to those in need. So large groups of people emigrated. In the month of May the number of those who had crossed the channel was 7,000. In the Netherlands, then and later, those emigrants were called only "Palzer' [for the German 'Pfälzer,' as people from the Pfalz].

"Several weeks after the edict of the Kurfürst, the area of the Weierhof was given to the principality of Naussau-Weilburg.[14] Now the most difficult times were past. The Fürsten [princes] of Nassau were more friendly toward the Mennonites than the Kurfürsten [electoral princes] of the Palatinate, and were glad to have them as capable farmers. Now they did not have to worry anymore about bad harvests, hail, or fire, or that they could not meet the obligations of the lease, because if there were unusual circumstances their obligations were reduced. The princes of Nassau were well disposed in general toward the Mennonites, but in particular to those living at the Weierhof. How that happened you will learn when I tell you the story of your uncle, my oldest son Michel.

"Even when he was a little boy, he was quite a 'Bosler and Tüpfler' [in English this may mean that he was a mischievious person and lived carelessly]. When he grew up he learned a trade at Möllinger's, a master watchmaker in Neustadt. Our Michel learned his trade cheerfully and enthusiastically, and pretty soon knew all about the crafts o f watchmaking, becoming a reliable Geselle [traveling journeyman— as a Geselle, any craftsman, to learn more in his trade, spent a period of years as an itinerant apprentice]. Three years then he was wandering in the region. When he came to a master who didn't know very much, he quickly packed his bags again and kept on wandering. But if he came to a place where he could learn something new, he would stay there, and he was always well liked. When he finally returned from his wandering years, his good master Möllinger had died. He now took on the business for the widow of master Möllinger. Because he had learned his trade well, the customers were coming from everywhere, and the business was better than at the times of the old master Möllinger.

"Around that time the Fürst Karl Christian moved his residence from Weilburg to Kirchheim. Among other pieces of art, Karl Christian had a wonderful clock. When, for example, it was striking 12 o'clock, a little door opened and the twelve apostles would appear and pass by slowly. There was something broken in this clock. Many watchmakers had already tried their luck, but none of them was able to get it going again. When our Michel heard about this, he went on his way to Kirchheim. With God's help, he was able to repair this clock, and after a few days it was just as accurate as before. The young princess was beside herself with joy, when at the stroke of twelve the apostles appeared again for their procession. Also the Fürst was very pleased, and gave our Michel the personal freedom to do his trade, and urged him to settle down in Kirchheim, where he wanted to have such a s killed man closer to him.

"Michel was only there for a few days when one morning he left his fine workshop to deliver a new clock. When he stood under the doorway he remembered that he had forgotten something and he quickly turned around, but can you imagine his horror when he saw what appeared to be himself sitting at the table being busy with a clock. He approached this image and looked across the shoulder of his alter ego, and there he saw how the second finger was pointing towards the clock, close to the number 12.

"The following morning Michel had to stay in his bed and he had a high fever with hallucinations. The prince sent his personal physician, but even his skill was not sufficient to save the life of the patient. After two days he was dead.

"By special permission from the prince, it was permitted that he was buried at the city cemetery.[15] Cousin Adam preached at his funeral as I never heard anyone preach before. Among those attending the funeral were members of the princely family. There also was the widow of the master Möllinger of Neustadt and her only daughter Judith, a lovely girl, Michel's fiancée. She had hoped that she soon would be led to his home as his wife, but now she was standing at his graveside. She was so broken in her sorrow that she simply could not be consoled. But her mother said, 'Judith, Judith, don't be a pagan [she should accept God's judgment].'

"From that time on the princes were still friendlier and were looking for ways to make it easier for us. In general, they tried their best to heal the wounds of war which had exhausted their land. They were supportive of agriculture, and lifted the raising of animals to a higher level by importing animals from Switzerland. So through the efforts of the princes of Kirchheim, their land became one of the most beautiful in all of Germany.

"There was only one thing we had to complain about very much: the many wild animals which the princes let roam freely everywhere. Whole herds of deer and wild pigs were destroying the land for agriculture. During the night we had to stand on guard to watch our fields, chasing those animals away. They had refuge in the middle of our fields, in the two Remisen [special preserves].[16] To enter this refuge area to pursue the animals was punishable by death. At the fields which were in the middle of the woods there was still greater damage that we had to endure, and woe to those who even had the thought of killing or wounding any of the wild animals. Cousin Rupp from the Heubergermill can tell about this. He had a servant who was hunting pheasants during the night, and one evening he also convinced Rupp's youngest boy to go with him. They took lights and went together into the woods. But someone told about them. So the servant was put into prison in Weilburg, the son had to leave the country, and the father had to pay a high money penalty.

"For many peasants this was an unbearable situation. From Sippersfeld and Breunigweiler, for example, many emigrated for that reason to Poland. But this has changed for the better now. When four years ago our current prince Friedrich Wilhelm, whom God may bless, took command, he immediately ordered that the wild animals in these refuges should be killed.

"Also in the matter of religion the princes of Nassau gave the Mennonites more freedom. Soon after the Weierhof became a part of the principality of Nassau, a little congregation was formed which then joined the congregation of Erbesbüdesheim. If I remember correctly, the service was held alternately at Erbesbüdesheim and at the Weierhof. I know this much, that my uncle Christian Krehbiel was already here in 1718 as the person to take care of the poor. Around 1750 the Weierhof became a separate congregation, joined by brethren in the faith living in the area. The Kägys and the Stauffers from the Bolanderhof, the Ellenbergers from Otterbergerhof in Rüssingen, the Danners from the Donnersberg and Neuhof, the Kägys from Gundheimerhof, the

The open (east) side of "Adamshof," or "Mittlehof" (home in the middle between the homes on higher ground and the home at the Mill on lower ground a Weierhof). One of the renovations or additions to this home may have been done in 1770, since that date has been found carved on an outer beam during recent renovations. It was here that ministers Christian Krehbiel and Valentine Krehbiel were born. In 1851, they came to America with their parents and eventually settled in central Kansas. Credit: David Habegger.

Haurys from Froschhauerhof, the Brubakers from Münchhof in Albisheim, and the Eymanns in Bennhausen.[17]

"The first preacher of the congregation was my father-in-law Moritz Ellenberger from Rüssingen, and the one who cared for the poor at that time was Abraham Künzi from here. We held our service at the home of Jost Krehbiel, the father of cousin Adam. And soon the little room was too small. In 1770 we began to build a church. We were in the midst of doing so when an order came from the Prince Karl Christian of Kirchheim to immediately stop the activity. Being too trusting in the Prince, we had neglected to get his permission to start with the building of the church, and the prince was very angry about this. But through a reconciliation by the Geheimrath de la Poitrie (a local official), it was possible to continue with the building of the church after payment of 53 fl. 12 kr. And still in the same year the church was dedicated by the preacher Jakob Galle from Uffhofen and Johannes Krehbiel from Wartenberg.

Going downhill through the yard between the home called "Adamshof" and its barns, one enters another courtyard. To its left, one can glimpse the home called "Ulis" or "Unterhof," or "By the Mill," so named ater Ulrich Krehbiel, the father whose children listened to tales by their grandfather in this story, and also named by its relation just above the low-lying home at Weierhof called "The Mill." Credit: Howard E. Krehbiel.

"Now I have told you a lot of things. Tomorrow I will see who among you will remember most."

And the children exclaimed, "We will remember everything! We will never forget."

In France revolution had broken out. In the beginning noble people like Klopstock and Schiller considered the revolution as the dawning of better times, and greeted it with enthusiasm. But when all human and divine order had been thrown over once again, and when the

Parts of adjacent barns nearly hide the tiny Mennonite Church built at the village of Weierhof in 1770. This was the first church that the people of the community were permitted to build, and even then permission required that it be unobtrusive in appearance, as if it were related to the barns. The cemetery behind this church was first used soon after 1770. Burial plots in the tiny cemetery are later reused for later burials, the stones made available to living relatives, or gently stored nearby, as is the case in most graveyards of Germany and Switzerland. Credit: Howard E. Krehbiel.

King had to die under the guillotine, and mass murder once again became the order of the day, then they turned away with disgust from these cruel scenes and didn't want to have anything to do with these subhuman bands of people. Wild masses of people were turned loose, and with animal-like roughness, they were tearing the remnants of their kings from their graves at St. Denis and they destroyed their remains by throwing them in a pit together with the bones of animals—including those of the king in whose name 100 years earlier the Palatinate had been devastated. And they also laid to ruin the imperial graves in the Cathedral of Speier.

Looking from near the 1770 Weierhof Mennonite Church westward down Crayenbühlstrasse (past the manure pile by the front entrance to one of the oldest homes), toward "Adamshof" named for famous Mennonite minister, Adam Krehbiel, whose ministry the first church was built. Credit: Howard E. Krehbiel.

The grandfather did not live to see this judgment of God. On July 11, 1792, he was called to his ancestors. Some months later the French were moving under Custine, coming from Weissenburg [Wissemburg on the northern border of Alsace] into the Palatinate, took Speier, Landau, Worms, and on October 21, they also took the unprotected fortress of Mainz. Again everywhere things were put to fire, and the Weierhof was not forgotten. But the French had only begun their devastations when they were chased out again by the Prussians under General Kalkreuth. In 1794 the Palatinate was again occupied by the French. During all these changing events the Weierhof remained comparatively untouched. People from the Weierhof had to be sent to work at the fortifications of Mainz which was beseiged by the French, and they also had to send food there. At that time, the Weierhof itself was not destroyed. However, that did happen when in 1796 the

Looking east along the narrow Crayenbühlstrasse between homes built in the 1830s toward some of the older homes of the Weierhof village that were initially built in the late 1690s and early 1700s. Credit: Howard E. Krehbiel.

French had to retreat from the army of Archduke Karl [son of the emperor of Austria?]. Anything that was not tied down was taken away. Some took even the clothes from people's bodies. Also the church was ruined and the chairs were broken, and the little box with the gifts was stolen. What they couldn't take along in food, they destroyed, so they, for example, cut to ribbons the beds and they strewed the feathers over the fields. Soon after, the whole left bank of the Rhine was given to France. Then also the Weierhof, in addition to the normal war taxes and other costs, and taxes for the care of the sick, had to make further payments.

But now it is time to see what happened to the family which the teller of this story has introduced earlier. With concern this family looked towards the year 1805 in which the young man Heinrich reached the age for compulsory military duty. Encouraged by the good success of two assemblies of preachers and the church elders from the Rhine and the area of the Neckar River which took place at Ibersheim,[18] a third assembly was called in 1805 to the Weierhof, to discuss a petition to the

French government concerning conscription. But the proud Emperor, who was boasting in Egypt to have destroyed the Cross, could not be expected to take into consideration special requests by his subjects regarding the faith.

What all were afraid of, happened. The Mennonites had to serve in the Army with weapons. Among them our Heinrich soon was called to the colors. It remains to the imagination of the reader to think of the heartache this caused among his relatives. All the people at the Weierhof expressed their concerns and many went some way with him and said goodbye to him—never to see him again.

What Heinrich had to experience one can read in general from his letters, which through the goodness of his brother, a grand-father of high age, have been made available to the teller of this story. I want to share some of these letters in their entirety, and excerpts from others.

*   *   *

Lille, 3 July 1805

Dearest parents and brothers and sisters!

I hope that this letter will find you in good health, and to have this confirmed by you would give me great pleasure. As far as I am concerned, I am at Lille in the Northern Military District of Flanders, where I have been assigned to the 1st Company, 3rd Batallion, 46th Infantry Regiment of the Line Troops. We were marching for 25 days and used up most of our money because nothing was handed out to us, and most of the time we have been living in barns and stables. But now it is getting even worse because the French are not giving us any payments at all. One day we have peas, and on the next day we have beans. Everything here is very expensive; one can buy for 30 kreuzer here less than what we could get for 15 kreuzer at home. There is a rumor that we will not stay for long here, because our regiment is camping at Boulogne by the sea. Our daily drills last for five hours. As soon as we arrived here, our hair was cut according to the new French fashion. Those who fell ill during the march were put on wagons and then delivered to the hospitals. As far as my health is concerned, I am still well. Please accept my greetings, father and mother, brothers and sisters, and all good family friends, and in particular my comrades. I hope that

none of them will find himself in the situation that I am in
now; we have been treated, when we arrived here, like robbers.

I am your faithful son,
Heinrich Krehbiel

*   *   *

Im Lager zu Boulogne
sur mer 16thermidor 13

*[In camp at Boulogne by the sea, August 3, 1805; beauti-
ful ink sketches of ships in harbor are on the original letter.]*

Much beloved parents!

I am no longer at Lille. We are now at Camp Boulogne.
There are many people here. We are very close to the ocean.
We see the English ships cruising outside the harbor. Daily
there are French soldiers having exercises with ships. Nearly
every day we are losing people in small engagements. Recently the English lost three ships. I was told that the French
Emperor has been here, and a great parade has been held. He
was sitting on a high throne, and people had to march by
him. Also the ships paraded by the Emperor and gave their
salute. He distributed many decorations among his soldiers.
It is supposed to have been very impressive. If it just will
turn out well. I had to remember a story which I read some
time ago in a book which had been given to me by cousin
Adam. There was a king of Persia,[19] who was sitting on a
high throne, inspecting his whole fleet passing by, but then
he suffered a total defeat.

I have had my money changed to 2 carolins in Lille, and
lost in the process 6 livres. Did you get my letter from Lille?

I greet you all, father, mother, and sisters and brothers,
and I

am your faithful son
H. K.

*   *   *

Heilbrunn, 1 October 1805

Dear parents and brothers and sisters!

Your letter of July 15 arrived here on September 29, and

I can see from it that you, thank God, are still well. As far as I am concerned, I am also still in good health. On July 30 we moved away from the ocean and until today we have been marching along. There were 200,000 of us that have been crossing the Rhein. Now we are near Heilbrunn in camp. Since we have crossed the Rhein, we always have to camp out in the open. Any day now we could be in battle. I believe this time it will be very dangerous. I am asking God daily that He should maintain my health so that I could return home safely. I certainly would have to write much more, my dear parents, but today it is impossible. I don't have a bigger piece of paper.Only this little note, so you know where I am. You are writing that you have sent me a carolin. I did not receive it yet. Please don't send any more money until I write for it.

I remain your faithful son, even unto death.

H. K.

*   *   *

Strassburg, 9 March, 1806

God's blessings and greetings, my beloved parents and brothers and sisters!

Only a few lines. Since about ten weeks I am no longer with my regiment. Four hours from Brünn[20] I have been captured; I have been transferred to—[illegible], and from there to Prague. In Bohemia I took sick and have been feeling bad ever since. When we left—[illegible] we were assigned to the marching route to Strassburg. There I am now in the hospital.

Greetings to you all
H. K.
[Following this letter he has been visited from the Weierhof.]

*   *   *

Boulogne, 13 August 1806

My dear parents and brothers and sisters!

I am, thank God, again well. When we left Strassburg, I thought it would be a change to the better; but here at the

33

ocean it is much worse. Twice daily we have our drills, and every third day we are on night watch. But we don't get enough to eat, and we are paid only a little money. Until now we have to pay for our own clothes, and have to get them. The money you are writing about I still have not received. May be it will be possible to buy myself free from the Batallion. Let me know your opinion. There is nothing new to report, other than that there is much talk about peace with England, and that all is quiet on the oceans.

My greetings to all of you,

your H. K.

*　　　*　　　*

Berlin, 21 October 1806

My dear parents, brothers and sisters!

Since my last letter many things happened, but we don't know what will be next; that is only known by God. We were marching day and night and had to make great efforts. The whole Prussian Army in Germany, all their cavalry and infantry, have been completely destroyed, and all their strongholds, cannons, and flags are in our hands; that is, the fortifications of Erfurt, Magdeburg, Spandau, Küftrin, and Stettin. Now the Prussians retreated to Poland and united with the Russians. Hopefully, we will be as fortunate in the future. We had tough battles and many people were lost, but, thank God, I and also Steiber and Espenschied, have not been hurt. You will be so good to give this news to his parents. We had to keep on marching from Leipzig to Magdeburg, from there through Mecklenburg to Lübeck; from there again for 50 hours back to Berlin, where we had a rest of two days. That was my first opportunity to tell you how I am. Now we are on our way to Poland. There we will see whether God will lead us further on, as He was with us so far in all ways. I now conclude, and send you my greetings, and remain

your faithful son
H. K.

*　　　*　　　*

34

With comfort from God and Jesus as friend!
Most worthy parents and brothers and sisters!

I hope that these few lines will find you in good health. As far as I am concerned, I am not in good condition; I have a bad fever for the last seven days. I had to suffer much through this year; I took part in a great battle and did not get wounded. All in all, we have lost 50,000 men and many have been captured. The battle was in the 8th of February by Eylau in Prussia; it was even more heated than the Battle of Austerlitz. After the battle we retreated to Liebstadt, where we have been camping in the open field for the past 3 months. There is much suffering in this land. Eylau and several villages are burned down. Everything is very expensive here. A bottle of beer costs 20 kreuzer, a glass of brandy 30 kreuzer, a pound of bread 56 kreuzer, a bottle of wine 3 1/2 florin. The horses are grazing out in the cornfields because we have no other supplies. Even the straw from the roofs has been used for the horses.

I received your letter from Mainz, but the carolin was not in it.

I send you many greetings and remain your

H. K.

*   *   *

In his following letter, dated July 29, 1807, he writes that he is still in hospital to recover from his fever, and that his health is improving. He has received two karolin which we had sent. On January 1, 1808, he sent new year greetings from Boulogne to his parents, and remarks that he has received their letters, but not the four louisdor which were said to be in it.

*   *   *

Vitoria, 8 May 1808

Dear parents and brothers and sisters!

We marched over 300 hours to Spain. The city of Vitoria, where we are now, is more than 400 hours of marching time away from you. Thank God I am healthy, which I also hope to be the case with you. It is not good with food around here; all we get is Welsh corn bread. Some say that we might go to Portugal to sail from there to England. Recently I saw the King and Queen of Spain and their son; they were here on their way to Bayonne, where the Emperor of France currently resides. I saw him also when we were marching, this "Napoleon, by the Grace of God and the Constitution, Emperor of France and the Protector of the Confederation of the Rhein," as he calls himself. He is a little man, with a dark expression in his face. I had to think when I saw him, is that really the man who can make the world tremble and who makes the kingdoms shake?

If you have the opportunity, please tell Schalles in Dahlsheim that his son is still well.

I am greeting all of you, your faithful

H. K.

*   *   *

This was the last letter which the parents received from their son. Over three years they did not hear from him. In September 1811, they received the following letter from Dahlsheim, which a comrade of Heinrich had sent home.

*   *   *

Villavicencia province
de Leon en Castille,
12 August 1811

Dear parents!

I am, thank God, still alive; but my comrades, nearly all of them, have died or are in hospital. Recently I also had a shot wound on my left arm. We were commissioned to cover a courier service. But when we came through a little forest we suddenly were attacked by a band of robbers. Many of us were killed or captured; comrade Krehbiel fell dead right next to me. We were only able to save ourselves through a quick retreat. We have very hard times here; we always have to be very watchful. There is no day, no hour, when one can feel safe from the enemy. A pastor[21] is supposed to be their leader. But the worst lot is for him who is being captured; then they

36

kill all prisoners in the most cruel ways. We also don't give any pardon anymore. Anyone who comes into our hands will be cut down. We only left a few Monks alive; we make them carry our baggage. Sometimes I feel sorry for them; but when I think what they have done to our comrades, I also help beating them up.

I have already written three letters and have received no replies. Send greetings to the Krehbiel at the Weierhof and tell him that his son has been shot to death.

Greetings from your son

Konrad Schalles

*   *   *

A few months later the French were certain of victory and were moving proudly toward new conquests on the newly built Emperor's road. They had as their commander of this great army the glorious Emperor himself, who thought he would lead them to new victories and new honors. Also the youth from Weierhof hurried to Marnheim to see the fine mounted regiments passing through. Some Chasseurs [carriages] galloped ahead of the unit and drivers talked to the surprised people in the village on both sides of the road. But nobody could understand what they were saying. When they came close to our young people, Christel Jakob, who had a certain knowledge of French, heard them ask repeatedly the question: "On est la route de Mayence?" (Wo is der Weg nach Mainz?) [Which is the road to Mainz?]. And he moved forward and showed them the way with the words "Voici a route de Mayence, messieurs!" (Hier is der Weg nach Mainz, meine Herren) [Here is the way to Mainz, gentlemen]. After they had gratefully shaken hands with him, they moved on, followed by the magnificent horsemen.

And one year later the French came back on the same road but in the opposite direction, and they were torn to pieces and in terrible shape, sick and without hope, and carrying along with them terrible epidemic diseases. In their midst there were some prisoners who hardly could move on from exhaustion. The people seeing this wanted to give them something to eat and to drink, but the French pushed them back rudely. And because it was in the autumn, they dumped several baskets of apples on the street so that the poor prisoners could pick them up in passing by. As soon as one of them would bend down, he would feel the gun shaft in his ribs, so they passed by, a picture of horror and pity.

Another army followed, from whose lips strange and unaccustomed sounds were heard, and with whom the knowledge of the French language was of no use for Jakob. It was the Russian Army that followed the retreating French. Over 100 cossacks took quarters for several days at the Weierhof. They were an amusing lot, content and satisfied if they got only sauerkraut and schnapps. The latter had to be fetched in buckets from the basement and shared out among the bearded warriors. Some of them took all too many liberties with the women. One would call to their attention that this is not proper, but they did not want to seem to understand it. Then one of our elders went to the Colonel about this, while he was lodging in Marnheim. This Colonel invited him to come to his room where he was quietly lying on his bed, and showed his back to his visitor while he listened to his complaints. As soon as he heard what the reason for the complaint was, he jumped out of his bed and dressed himself in the presence of our elder. When arriving at the Weierhof, we had to point out the soldiers concerned to him, and without much hesitation, he gave them a rough treatment with his fists. One soldier was bound, because of his behavior, to the wheel of a wagon standing in the fields, and there he had to spend the long winter night. There also were some comical scenes. One of those is told in a poem with the title:

"Die Russische Stiefelwichse"
[The Russian high boot polish]

Hear, my friend! What I am telling you
Happened in the war.
When the Allies achieved victory
Over the French Army,
When they overcame Napoleon,
This horrible man
Who knew no limits,
And who thought he was invincible,
But who to live out his days,
Found himself on a quiet island.
In this war now
There was Russia's brave army
Fighting to the end,
Absorbing at the same time
More and more of our customs.

38

Also in the world of fashion
The Northmen did not stay behind.
They eagerly caught up
With French manners,
Which they had not practiced
As long as they were living at home.
So it happened
That a Russian wanted to polish his boots,
And did not know what material to use.
He had no knowledge of real shoe polish.
But soon he seemed to be very happy.
He found at our basement door
The black grease which we use
For smearing our wagon wheels.
And the good fellow thought
That this would be the shoe polish;
Without much hesitation
He applied this stuff
To his big riding boots.
Then he walked grandly back and forth,
Looked at his boots again and again
And was bursting with pride;
There was one problem—
The so-called shoe polish stank frightfully.

*   *   *

Before the departure of the Russians, there was very mild weather. Movement from house to house was possible only through deep mud; with boards we had to fix up temporary walkways. When the Russians left, one of them, probably filled with too much schnapps, virtually disappeared in the mud, and those that followed him stepped right over him. But then another wagon followed, and a man picked up this man who was covered completely with dirt and half senseless, put him on his wagon, and on they went into France.

With the Russians also other things disappeared. In particular, much yarn, which they used to mend their boots. What they did take with them was easy to replace; but what they left behind was of disastrous consequences. The French when fleeing from the Russians had brought into the land the disease of typhus, which then also demanded numerous victims at the Weierhof. One of the first ones was Jakob Krehbiel, who had served as pastor for twelve years with a rare faithfulness and much sincerity, just as his grandfather Adam Krehbiel. The whole congregation, who honored him with loving affection, were praying that his life should be spared; but God had decided otherwise. Only 35 years old, and after 16 days of illness, he passed into the joys of the Lord on December 6, 1813. A grave was prepared in the new cemetery which he had helped to originate.[22]

Soon the cemetery filled up with graves. On March 8, 1814, also the soldier Heinrich's father Ulrich died; of his ten children, five had preceded him into eternity. Sensing the closeness of his death, he himself put together his testament. The reader who has followed this narrative so far probably would like to have knowledge of his testament, which reads as follows.

*　　　　*　　　　*

Weierhof, 3 December 1813

When our elder father became old and tired of life, weak and ill, he gathered his children around him and said: "I will die, and God will be with you," and he blessed them. Because I, Ulrich Krehbiel, now nearly 59 years old, do not know know how near my end is; and because I cannot know whether I, like our elder father, will be fortunate enough to talk to my children on my death bed, I thought that I should, being of good health now, put down my will in writing to my beloved wife and my children.

Now I think I will die rather soon. And, by the grace of God, you, my dear wife, and you, my children, will survive me. So I say in the words of our elder father: "I will die and God will be with you," and I beg from the almighty God that he will have mercy upon you. He shall spread his wings of grace over you, and send his holy angels that they will watch over you and keep you, particularly from any damage to your bodies and souls. I beg that God through his grace will bless your thinking and your words, your doings and your omissions, your going in and going out.

Now my beloved wife, my faithful companion, I am certain that as long as God will keep you healthy, that after my death you will follow your work faithfully as you have done. Nevertheless, I admonish you and beseech you, that our children shall continue to be brought up in prayer and to do good; and that they will avoid bad company and will not fall for bad morals. Search, for as long as you live together, to do your work in peace and unity together, so God will also be with you.

And you, my dear children, be obedient and follow your mother; she will have only good advice for you. The holy spirit will lead you and guide you, that you may conduct a God-pleasing and pious life. Have always before you the all-seeing and all-knowing one, and avoid sin, so that God and his holy angels will be with you. If you should choose to live in the desires of your eyes and of your flesh, you will have bad spirits surrounding you; even as the king Saul was disobedient to God, the evil spirits came over him. And as soon as Judas betrayed our Saviour, the Devil was entering him; from all these things God wants to keep us in his grace.

So continue to walk as it is proper before the all-seeing and all-knowing God, as you hope to be walking some day in eternity, and as you would like to remember to have lived when you were here upon this earth. Therefore be watchful and pray, and search diligently in the scriptures. If you have time, read also the pious books where you will find many rewarding things which are also useful for your soul and body.

Now you, my dear children who have married already and who have children, search in prayer for your children to do good, and remind them and warn them from evil companionships. And those of you my dear children who are still alone, remember that you should unite in marriage, but that when you will do so, that you ask God that he should give you faithful and virtuous husbands or wives that you might live a pious, God-pleasing life. If the Lord will bless your work, be also kind, merciful and friendly to the poor and neglected, and those who suffer great needs. If you have much, give much; if you have little, so give as much as you can. Grace be to him who cares for the needy, and our Lord will watch over him in bad times.

So my wish for you now is that you all love each other, be faithful and in friendship according to the teaching of our Lord Jesus. O, that all people might live that way; the world would not be such a sad valley of burdens, we would have no wars and destruction would not take place any longer. Since we however are still living in a sad and terrible time, and since we cannot know whether enemy or friends will take our possessions from us, I do not want to write about what will be left in material things at my death; but I wish that God will keep severe judgments from you in his grace and that he will protect you and keep you and guide you until through his grace and after our short term of life and through the merits of his Son he will lead you eventually into his glory.

And to you, my merciful God, I say praise and thanks for your grace, goodness, love, and faithfulness which you have shown me from my early childhood on. You have protected me from a thousand perils; I was ill only a few days, and I did not break my legs or arms at any time. Yes, you have taken care of me through your goodness that I suffered neither hunger nor thirst, so that I must say,"I have not been worthy of all your mercifulness and faithfulness which you have shown your servant." O, you great and merciful God, have mercy with me for Christ's sake, your beloved Son, and through the sacrifice of his blood he has forgiven all my sins of omission and of choosing evil rather than doing good. Also be with my children, and yes, all people, merciful and gracious, and forgive us all our sins, and cleanse our hearts from what we have done wrong, so that your spirit can dwell in us with strength, and that all our thinking, speaking, doing, and not doing, shall be according to your holy will and pleasure, so that when our course comes to an end, we, through your grace, will be led into eternal glory, in the name of Jesus Christ our Lord. Amen.

Now I want to leave this life,
If it so pleases God,
Willingly and with pleasure.
And I do not want to be sad,
Because in the wounds of Jesus
I have found my salvation.
And my comfort in the hour of death
Will be the death of you, Lord Christ.

So take now, Lord, at the end of my days
My soul into your hands.
Yes, let me come with all the faithful
Before your throne in Heaven,
That I may honor and praise you
In your glory through all eternity.

After that war a new period started at the Weierhof. The system of serfdom, of one person having proprietary rights over another, was terminated; many of the taxes for the land were changed, and the permission to use the land was gradually changed into the rights of ownership. About that time we also see even in writings the disappearance of the old simplicity and firmness of character which were the earmarks of people then, being replaced with easy-going and more casual writing, which reminds more of the French unsteady and superficial character. Before that time we found clothes and linens which had spun into them prayers and songs from a pious homemaker, and which had been done by hand in the houses, and which were passed on from generation to generation unchanged. But after that time and still today [1882] we find much lighter materials produced under the superficial methods of unsatisfied factory workers, then sold by the Jews, one day shaped in this manner and next day in that, and after a short time ending up on the garbage pile of the paper factory.

In earlier days—and the teller of this story does not want to just praise the good old times knowing that man regardess of whether he has homemade clothes or other clothes can be happy either way. So the teller of this story wishes that all his dear readers, on the big day of decision, will appear in clothes as the little poem says:

Christ's blood and justice,
That is my ornament and my garment.
In it I want to face my God
When I will go to Heaven.

View of Weierhof today. The old part of the village is on the left, the Mennonite school is in the center, and the apartments to the right were built by the U.S. Air Force. Credit: David Habegger.

Looking down the street into the present-day village of Weierhof from the direction of the Weierhof School. Credit: Howard E. Krehbiel.

CHILDREN AND GRANDCHILDREN
OF PETER KREHBIEL I
OF WEIERHOF

Compiled by
Howard E. Krehbiel

Peter Krehbiel I , b ca 1630/35, probably Zäziwil, Switzerland, d 1697? at Weierhof
    m (I) ca 1655/60 (name not known)
    m (II) ca 1665 **Anna** _____ , b ? , d Mar. 25, 1724 at Weierhof.
    This is the Peter Krähenbühl who is said to have been forced to leave the Swiss village of Zäziwyl by Grosshöchstetten in Canton Bern in 1671, and after living at several locations is known to obtain an inheritance lease

dated Feb. 2, 1682 of the land and buildings of the Weierhof other than the mill Feb. 2, 1682. In that document that still is displayed in the Klaus Galle home at the Weierhof his name is spelled Crayenbuhl by the official. Much has been written about this family, including the probability that one of Peter's brothers was the Jost Krehbiel who settled by 1709 at the Pfrimmerhof.

The children of Peter I and his first wife were:

1. **Ulrich**, b ca 1660, d Feb. 17, 1724, m (I) Barbara Widmer, m (II) Maria Hege, lived in the middle of the three upper homes, called "Mitteloberhof," later "Neuhannes."

2. **Peter II**, b ca 1655/1662, d Nov. 24, 1725, m (I) Magdalena Eicher, m (II) Maria Hunsicher, lived in the home called "Mittelhof," later to be called "Ins Adams."

Children of Peter I and Anna his second wife were:

3. **Johannes (Hans)**, b ca 1665/70, d before Feb. 25, 1715, m ca 1685/96 Christina Ellenberger who on the above date married Hans Jakob Kasper. Johannes lived in the upper home to the east called "Ins Hannes," "Althanneshof," later "Galles am Berg."

4. **Christian (Christel)**, b ca 1670/75, d 1744/46, m ca 1685/95 to ?, lived in the upper home to the west, called "Christelhof," "Ins Christels," later "Ins Gobels."

5. **Michael**, b ca 1685/6, d before 1749/50, m ca 1707/15 Anna ?, lived in the home lower down the hill (near the Mill) called "Unterhof," later to be known as "Ulis."

6. **a son**
7. **a daughter**
8. **a daughter**

[There may have been earlier children. Also, the name and data on the last son and two daughters is not well established so is not written here, though it is known that they were living when the 1685 census of Anabaptists of the region was taken.]

The stone erected in 1982 at the entrance to the village of Weierhof in commemoration of the 300th year since Peter Krehbiel first obtained his lease.

1. Ulrich Krehbiel I, b ca 1655/60 Zäziwil, Canton Bern, Switzerland, d Feb. 17, 1724, married (I) ca 1680 **Barbara Widmer,** b ca 1660, d one week before Mar. 14, 1717, and Ulrich married (II) ca 1717 **Maria Hege (Hoegren ?),** b ca 1685, d after July 10, 1739.

Ulrich became inheritance leaseholder in 1707 of the one fifth of the Weierhof called at different periods "Ins Ulrichs," "Mitteloberhof," and "Neuhanneshof," which had been constructed about 1683/4, burned 1697, rebuilt by 1707.

Little is known about most of his children. Children of Ulrich I and Barbara were:

> **11. Anna,** b ca 1680/85
> **12. Anna Elisabeth,** b ca 1680/85
> **13. Magdalena,** b 1680/85
> **14. Peter,** b ca 1685/95
> **15. Ulrich,** b ca 1685/95
> **16. Johannes** , b ca 1685/95, d Aug. 29, 1737

Children of Ulrich I and Maria were:

> **17. Katharina,** b after late 1717
> **18. Margaretha,** b 1724.
> The mother Maria and her daughters Katharina and Margaretha were still living at the time of the mother's leasehold division July 10, 1739.

2. Peter Krehbiel II, b ca 1655/1662, probably at Zäziwil, d Nov. 24, 1725, m (I) ca 1680/81 **Magdalena Eicher** of Erbesbüdesheim who d before 1690, m (II) ca 1685/90 **Maria Hunsicher.**

Peter II became in 1707 an inheritance leaseholder of the one fifth of the Weierhof called "Mittelhof" (not so far up the hill as others), later called "Adams Hof" or "Ins Adams," probably built or rebuilt by 1698, remodeled between 1740-45.

Children of Peter II and Magdalena were:

> **21. Anna,** b ca 1682, emigrated before 1725 to Pennsylvania, d before 1725.
> **22. Barbara,** b 1685, married twice at Rohrhof by Mannheim, d before 1725 in Pennsylvania.

Children of Peter II and Maria were:

> **23. Johannes,** b ca 1690/1700, ?
> **24. Fronica,** b ca 1690/1700, ? , lived 1725 in Primmelbach, district Germorsheim, Crown land of Weissenberg.
> **25. Johann Jost,** b ca 1695/1700, d 1742/43, m ca 1725/30 Anna Müller, b ca 1700, d Aug. 17, 1745, took over the parents' home. Later (1743) the widow Anna married a Heinrich Krämer.
> **26. Margarite,** b ca 1695/1705

Entry to the home called "The Mill" at Weierhof. Howard Krehbiel's great-grandfather, Jakob Krehbiel was born here and assisted his father, Jakob Krehbiel, in the 1830s with the task of designing and directing the building of the present-day Weierhof Church as well as four Weierhof homes of that era. Credit: Howard E. Krehbiel.

27. Daniel, b ca 1695/1705
28. Peter, b ca 1695/1705

3. Johannes (Hans) Krehbiel, b ca 1665/70, d before Feb. 25, 1715, m ca 1685/96 **Christina Ellenberger**, who on the above 1715 date m Hans Jakob Kasper.

Johannes became an inheritance leaseholder of 1/5 of the Weierhof, lived in the home called "Ins Hannese," "Althanneshof," later "Galles am Berg," built in 1682, burned in 1697, rebuilt by 1707.

Children of Johannes and Christina were:

31. Johannes (Hans), b ca 1685/1700, d before 1733, lived with his sister Barbara and her husband.

32. Michael, b ca 1700/10, m ca 1725/30 Anna Magdalena Rubel of Messerschwanderhof, lived as a farm manager on the Donnersberg.

33. a son, b before 1715, d before 1730.

34. Barbara, b ca 1700, m ca 1720 Johannes Kagy of Bolanderhof, who in 1720 obtained inheritance deed for the Weierhof Mill, also the "Althanneshof" and its land.

35. a daughter, b before 1715, d before 1730.

36. a daughter, b before 1715, d before 1730.

4. Christian (Christel) Krehbiel, b ca 1665/70, d after 1737, before 1746 at Weierhof, m ca 1685/95 _____.

Christian became inheritance leaseholder in 1707 of the one fifth of the Weierhof that became known as "Ins Christels". As one of the five sons of Peter Krehbiel I to remain at Weierhof, Christian is considered the builder of those five earliest homes and connecting barns, some of the originals of which were probably built by 1683, burned in 1697, then rebuilt by 1707. Already in 1718 he is known as the "Almozenpfleger," elder in charge of care of the disadvantaged of that Mennonite community.

Known children are:

41. Johannes, b ca 1695/00, d 1743, m ca 1730 Maria Kolb of Wolfsheim, b ca 1695/05, d 1750

42. Heinrich, b ca 1695/05, d ? , m ca 1728 Gertraud Lichti, widow of miller Johannes Ummel of Wartenberg and dau of miller Ulrich Lichti of Otterberg who earlier had the lease of the Wartenberg Mill from the Count of Wartenberg.

43. Johann Nikolaus, b ca 1695/05, d 1748, m ca 1720/30 Ursula Wohlgemuth of Eichenbacher Mill, and became miller there.

[Adolph Hertzler of the Gundheimerhof, now deceased, showed an old book to me in 1986 inwhich the recorded names suggest that there may also have been a daughter in this family named Barbara Krehbiel, wife of Rudolph Kägy of Oberwiesen.]

5. Michael Krehbiel I, b ca 1685/6 Weierhof, d before Oct. 25, 1752, m ca 1707/10 **Anna** ____, b ca 1680/90, d Dec. 24, 1757.

Michael was the youngest son of Peter Krehbiel I to obtain an inheritance lease of one fifth of the Weierhof. His section was called "Unterhof," "By the Mill," and later "Ins Ulis" or "Ulishof." One can still observe his carved initials "17 M K 12" on an outer beam on the upper side facing the path between the homes.

Their children:

51. Jakob, b ca 1710/15, lived in Pennsylvania by 1752, died there while living with a son Michael near York, PA before Dec. 5, 1791.

52. Heinrich, b ca 1715, d July 11, 1792, m ca 1748/50 Katharina

Ellenberger, dau of Ulrich Ellenberger and ___ of Ruessingen, lived in the parents home later called "Ulis."

53. **Michael II** , b ca 1717, d Feb. 7, 1785, m (I) ca 1743 Anna Barbara Eymann, m (II) after Oct. 1750 Katharina Eicher of Erbesbudesheim, lived at the Donnersbergerhof.

54. **Barbara**, b ca 1710/20, d ca 1771, m before Oct. 25, 1752 Heinrich Kramer of Weierhof, who lived at Weierhof as linenweaver at the "AltenHofhauschen;" no children.

55. **Susanna**, b ca 1710/20, d late 1785, m before Oct. 25, 1752 Jakob Zuerger who was miller at the Dannenfelser Mill; no children.

Adolph Hertzler (deceased in 1992), highly respected researcher of all Mennonite families in the proximity of Weierhof in Germany. Credit: Howard E. Krehbiel.

Looking down the lane from the north toward the farm called the Pfrimmerhof where Jost Krehbiel settled in 1709. This Jost is thought to be a brother of Peter Krehbiel who settled at the Weierhof in 1682 after they were forced to leave Switzerland in 1671. Credit: Howard E. Krehbiel.

A closer view of the older homes and barns of the Pfrimmerhof with its sur-rounding forest. Credit: Howard E. Krehbiel.

END NOTES

1. The narrator [Ellenberger] is sharing this poem as he found it, without altering the [Swiss/German] sentence structure and the spelling, as he did so when telling the life story.
2. Elector—one of the princes who was empowered to take part in the election of an emperor of the Holy Roman Empire of that time.
3. Hausser maintains in his excellent *History of the Palatinate*, Volume II, page 583: "The population of the Palatinate had dropped to 1/50 of its original size."
4. "The peaceful Anabaptists who had been living in the Palatinate for a century, and whose conversion was attempted in vain by Friedrich III, had been much bothered by Ludwig IV and his busy Lutheran counselors; one specific reference in the Palatinate law declared them to be not protected by the law. Karl Ludwig quietly eliminated this law, which had been a sign of Lutheran fanaticism. The Anabaptists were allowed to move into Mannheim, which had been entirely depopulated, provided that they would not continue in their heretic ways, and did live a normal business life in the city. And so it happened; in undemanding quietness they built up a small corporation led by their elders, which certainly was not to the disadvantage of life and activity in the town which recovered from its ruins; still today we can see remnants of these activities." (Hausser, page 587)

   Kurfürst Karl Ludwig enjoyed communication with the Mennonites. His daughter who was originally married to the Duke of Orleans, namely Elisabethe Charlotte, wrote in one of her very interesting letters that she well remembered the Mennonites of Mannheim, in whose workshops she often spent time when she was a little child.
5. The grandfather refers to the Peace of Nimwegen on the River Waal in 1678.
6. One Nassau official Johann Andrä recorded this in his books on genealogy of the persons of rank of Kirchheim and Stauf, as he wrote in about 1640: "Because of the demands of billeting requirements of military personnel and other destructive results of war in the years 1635-1639, nearly everywhere are found the locations of death from starvation and great distresses of war; the villages of Kirchheim, Orbis, Morschheim, Bischheim, Mittersheim, Albisheim, Rüssingen, and Dannenfels have become completely uninhabited."
7. The teller of the story almost has to be thankful to Louis XIV, because he would not have been able to report this interesting story if it had not been preserved in the archives in the city of Nassau as it happened about the May 1, 1683. The records there, called "De' nombrement de la Seigneucie de Kirchheim," are now [1882] to be found in the Provincial Archives at the city of Koblenz, and includes a short description of the municipalities belonging to this particular district. The narrator of this story feels great joy to find that the grandfather's story has been confirmed through the official documents.
8. Adam Krehbiel was the minister serving the congregation of the Weierhof from 1766 until his death in 1804. He preached the Word with great strength and joy, and the good news of reconciliaton with God. Teerstegen, whose writings have been read by many Mennonites, says about him, "He was a man according to the heart of God." And today [1882] he is living on, remembered by those who knew him. Letters by him [Adam Krehbiel] have been printed in the *Mennonitisches Blatter* of 1856, no. 3, in the *Palatinate Memorabile*, part II, page 201ff., and in the foreword of Teerstegen's *Weg der Wahrheit* [*Way of the Truth*].
9. For example, in Germersheim.

10. Even in the year 1800 there still was a Mennonite congregation in Berlin.
11. At Haag in Holland on October 30, 1697.
12. The narrator of this story remembers the famous Ryswick stipulation into which the French diplomats, during the night before the signing of the treaty, and probably upon the urging of the Kurfürst Johann Wilhelm, who was a Jesuit, had added ARTICLE IV which read: "However, the Roman Catholic religion must remain in all the areas concerned."
13. Whoever might be interested in this declaration of November 21, 1705 will find it printed in the *Palatinate Memorabile*, part III, page 95ff. In part I of the same document there is also the Mahnbrief [reminding letter] of the Kurfürst Friedrich III on page 164, which also is referred to in part II on page 86.
14. On January 30, 1706 the Count Johann Ernst of Nassau-Weilburg had given up several villages in return for the area of Bolanden. Belonging to the area of Bolanden was the village of Bolanden, with the Weierhof and the Bolanderhof; Marnheim, with the Froschauerhof; and Dreisen, with the Münsterhof.
15. At that time it was not permitted that Mennonites be buried in public places in the Palatinate, because they were of another confession. They had to buy their own places to bury their dead. Prof. Niel says in his well-known book, *Die Pfälzer [The Palatinate People]*, quite the opposite; however, his claim seems to be quite wrong.
16. Still today [1882] this area is called "in der Remise."
17. All these farms, as the historical records show, belonged to different monasteries in the middle ages. When they were secularized in the Reformation, many of these farms were given to the representatives of the monasteries, to counts and other noblemen. At the time when they were held by our ancestors, they were devastated in the war just like at the Weierhof, and the fields had not been cultivated, so that obviously was the task given by God to our ancestors.
18. At the first meeting, among other things, a rough draft of the proposal in the customary form of paragraphs was discussed and documented by Valentin Dahlem, the appointed preacher of the Mennonite congregation at Wiesbaden. The draft was presented to the second assembly for examination, and was found good and acceptable by the congregations of the Rhein area.
19. Probably it is Xerxes who is mentioned here in the Battle of Salamis.
20. In the Battle of Austerlitz (Bohemia).
21. Probably the "Pastor" Geronimo Merino, who was one of the first Guerilla leaders in the Old Castille.
22. It had been started in the year 1808, but work on it must have been interrupted, because the authorization of the prefect of Mainz was necessary; but this arrived only on June 16, 1810.

Index